soul asyl[um]
let your dim light shine

Transcribed by Bill La Fleur, Eli Simpson, Matt Scharfglass and Alex Houton

© 1995 WARNER BROS. PUBLICATIONS
All Rights Reserved

Editor: Aaron Stang
Transcription Editor: Colgan Bryan
Technical Editor: Glyn Dryhurst
Photography: Karen Mason
Art Design: Frank Milone / Joseph Klucar

CONTENTS

MISERY

Words and Music by
DAVID PIRNER

Verse 1:

and make_____ mis - er - y._____

Well I know just__ what you need, I might just__ have the thing.

*Bass plays D, E.

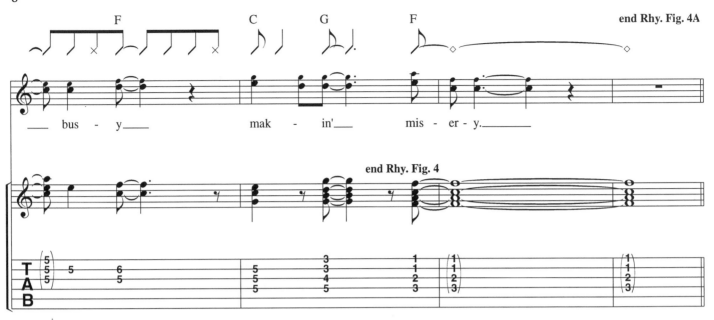

busy makin' misery.

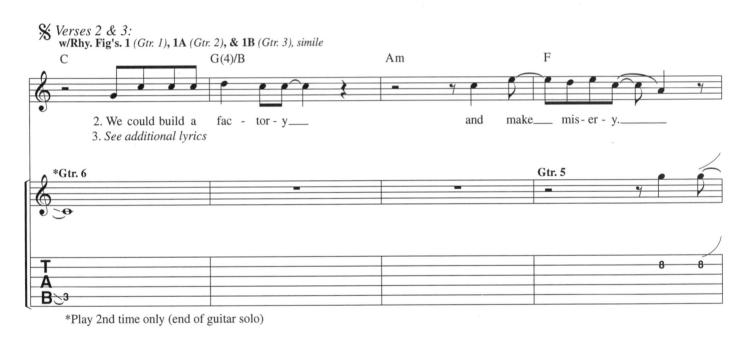

2. We could build a factory and make misery.
3. See additional lyrics

*Play 2nd time only (end of guitar solo)

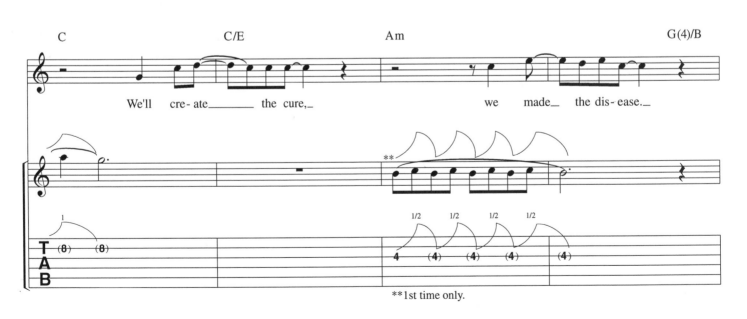

We'll create the cure, we made the disease.

**1st time only.

12

*Bass plays D.

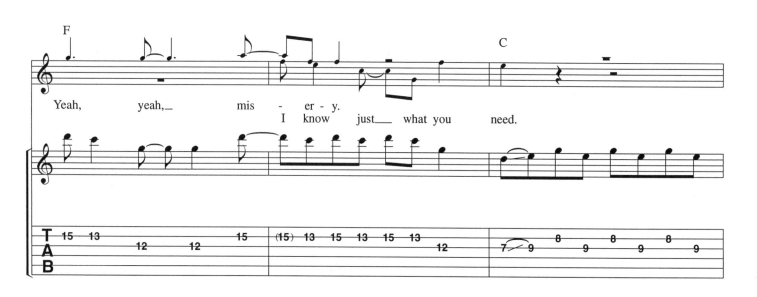

Verse 3:
Yet you satisfy your greed
Get what you need.
There's lonely envy,
So empty.

SHUT DOWN

By
DAVID PIRNER

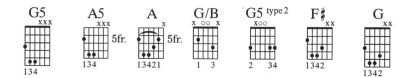

Shut Down - 8 - 1
PG9541

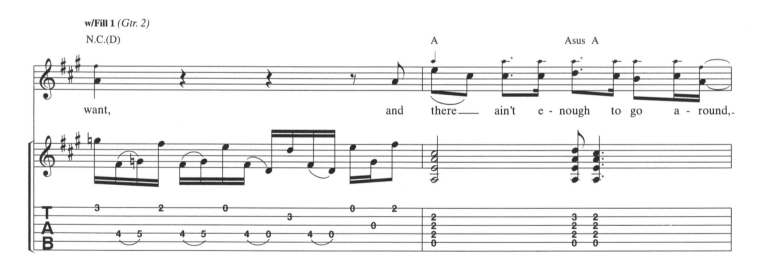

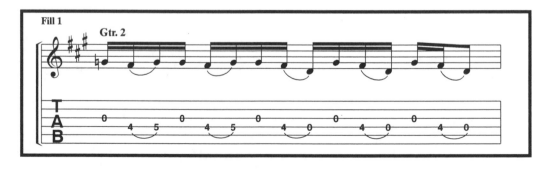

18

Shut Down - 8 - 5
PG9541

20

TO MY OWN DEVICES

By
DAVID PIRNER

26

HOPES UP

By
DAVID PIRNER

Hopes Up - 14 - 1
PG9541

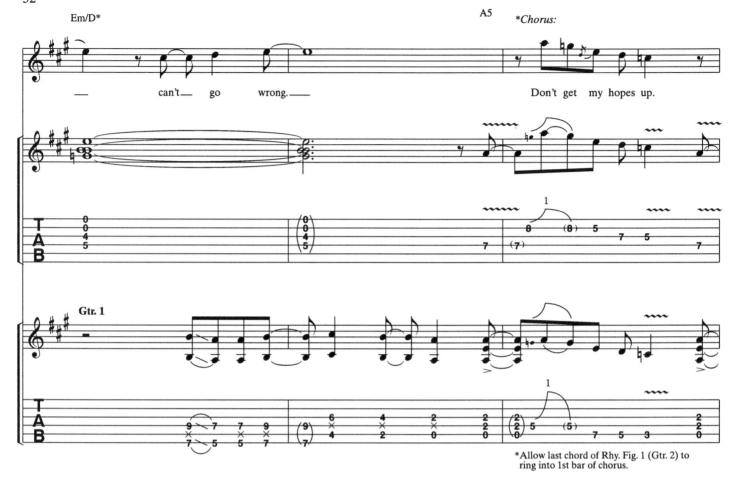

Em/D* A5 *Chorus:

can't go wrong. Don't get my hopes up.

Gtr. 1

*Allow last chord of Rhy. Fig. 1 (Gtr. 2) to
ring into 1st bar of chorus.

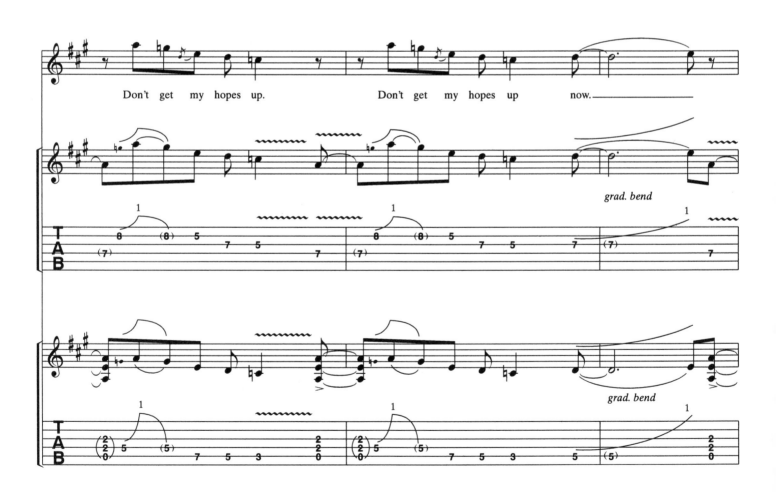

Don't get my hopes up. Don't get my hopes up now.

grad. bend

grad. bend

Don't get my hopes up. Don't get my hopes up. Don't get my hopes up now.

Verse 2:
w/Rhy. Fig. 1 *(Gtr. 2)*

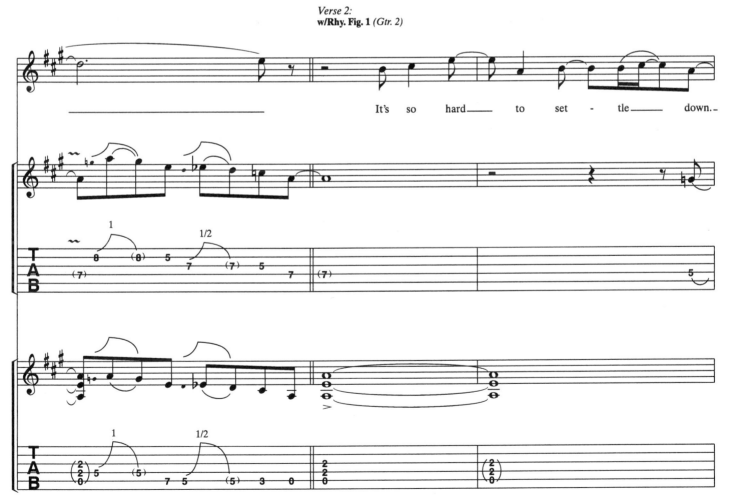

It's so hard___ to set - tle___ down.___

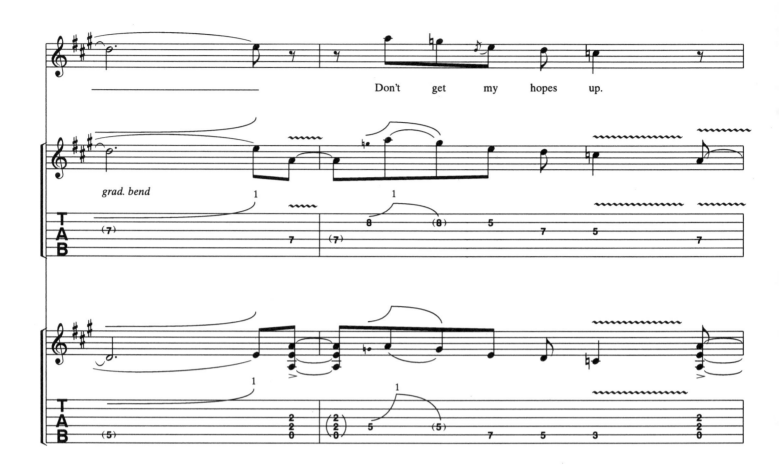

Don't get my hopes up.

Don't get my hopes up. Don't get my hopes up now. ____

38

Hopes Up - 14 - 10
PG9541

40

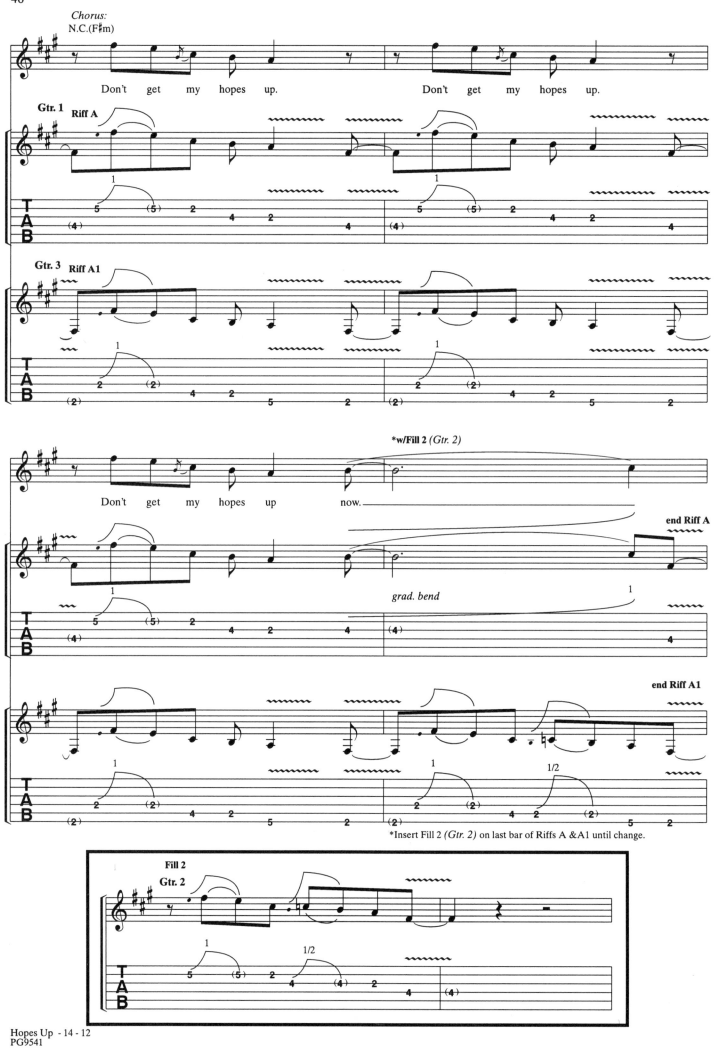

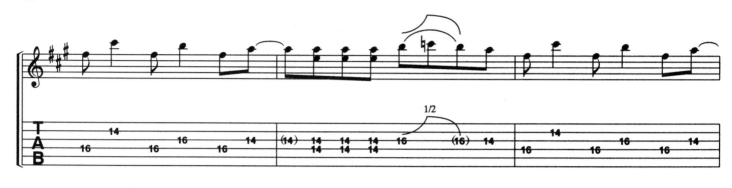

w/Riff A *(Gtr. 1, 1st 3 bars only)*

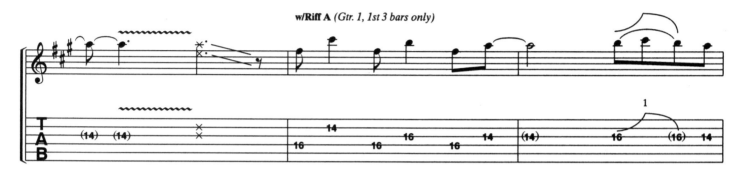

w/Fill 3 *(Gtr. 1)* **and w/Fill 4** *(Gtr. 2)*

*F#m7(♭5)

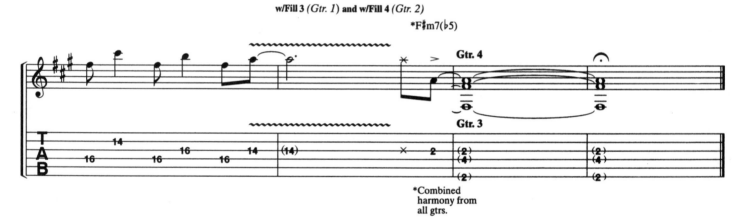

*Combined
harmony from
all gtrs.

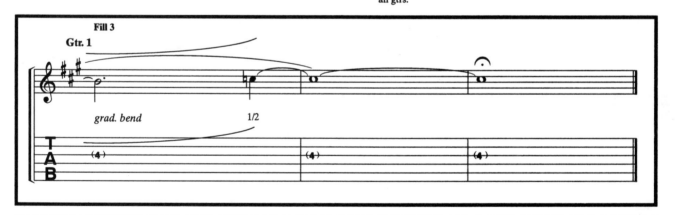

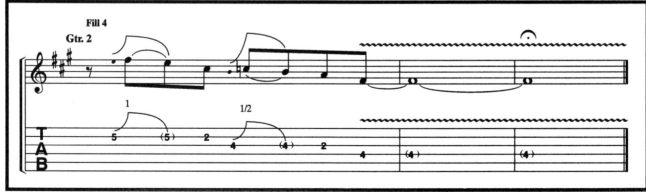

PROMISES BROKEN

By
DANIEL MURPHY and MARK PEARLMAN

Streets are filled— with bro-ken glass, you get bur-ied by the past,—

— give me just a lit-tle taste, lay— this mess to maste..

Take me home..

Verse 2:
w/Rhy. Fig. 2 *(Gtr. 3, simile)*

My mind is rac - ing, take me home,— my bod - y's ach - in', so a - lone,—

— I'll make you nan - na stay with me.— Be friend - ed by the en - e - my— one more

time. Ev - 'ry lit - tle thing a - bout this tells— me

Chorus:
w/Rhy. Fig. 1 *(Gtr. 2)*

Gtr. 3

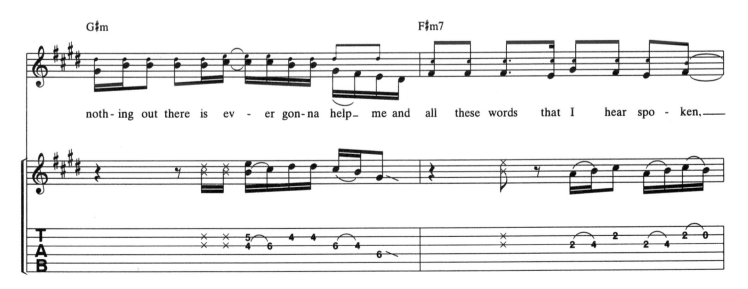

noth - ing out there is ev - er gon-na help— me and all these words that I hear spo-ken,—

46

just prom-is-es bro-ken now.

*Gtr. 4 overdub.

Bridge:

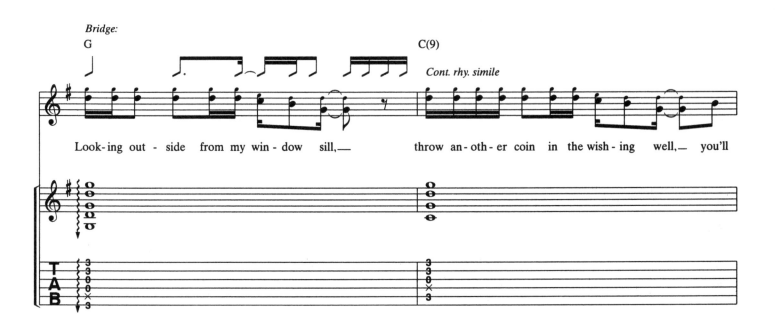

Look-ing out-side from my win-dow sill,— throw an-oth-er coin in the wish-ing well,— you'll

Cont. rhy. simile

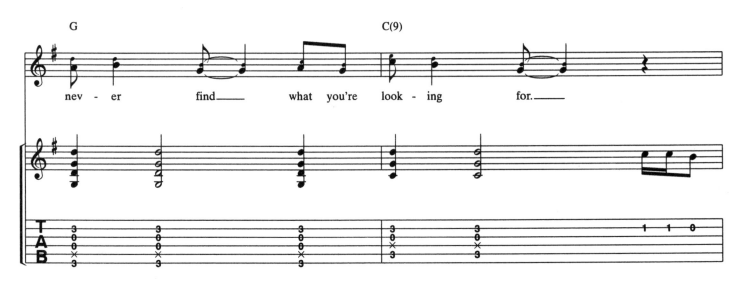

nev - er find___ what you're look - ing for.___

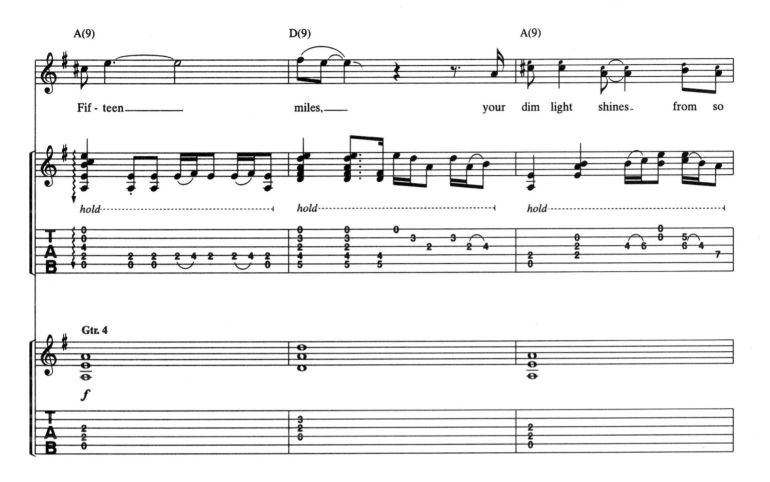

48

50

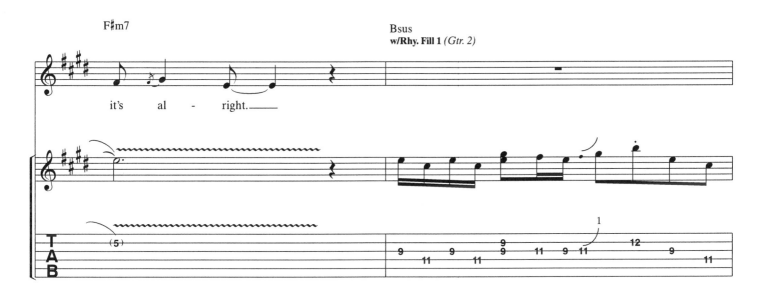

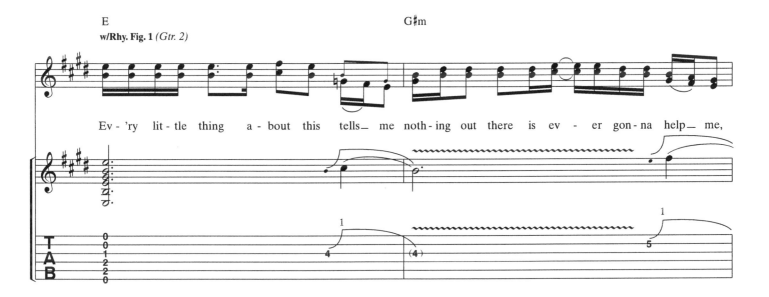

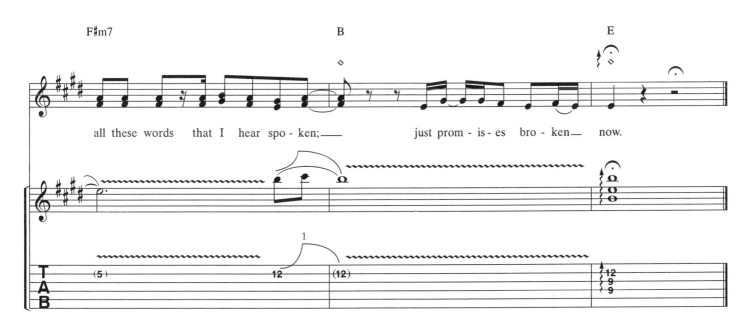

BITTERSWEETHEART

By
DAVID PIRNER

*All gtrs. ad lib. on Verse 2 a la Verse 1.

seeing eye dog— and I can't— ev-en see.— They're na-ked and they're fol-low-in' my

mas-ter who's blind— and my mind's gone to piec-es, I could use some piece of mind. So I

*Rhythms are approximate.
†Open strings sound sympathetically.

54

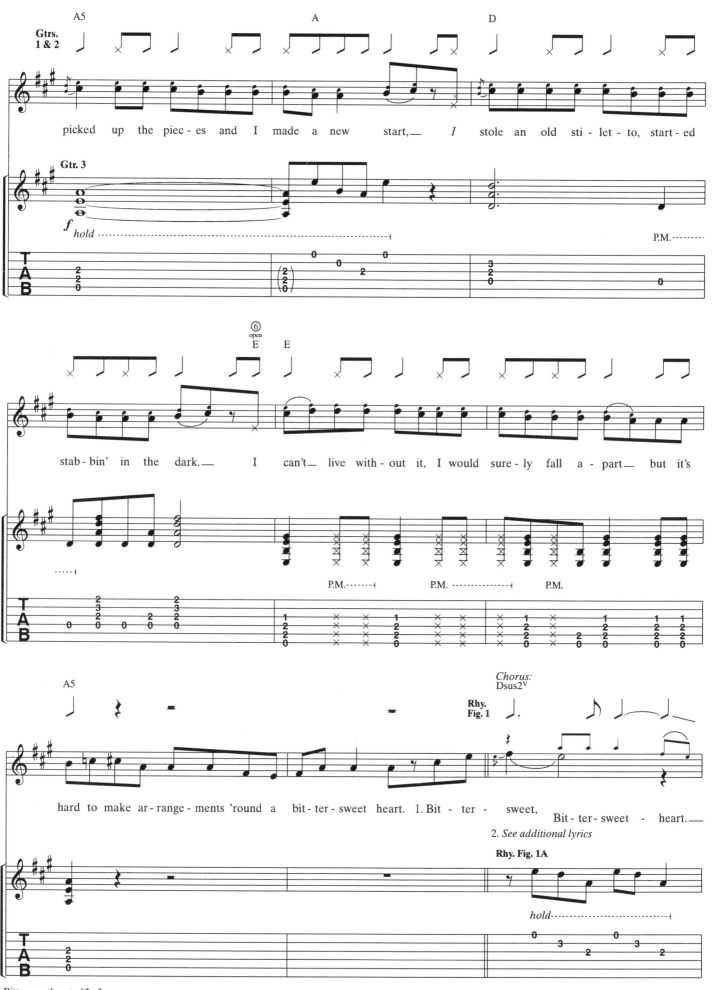

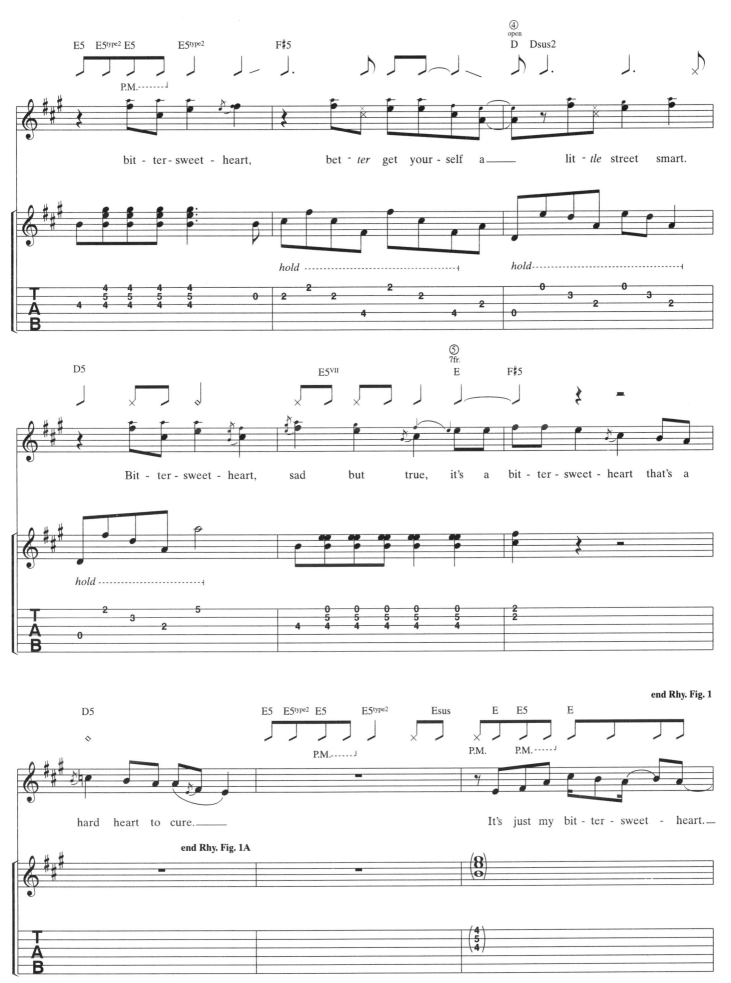

56

think just a drink might get you to the good part. Ly - ing in bed just a

won'- dring what to do, it's a bit - ter - sweet - heart— that's a hard heart to cure.____

In time in - side you find you al - ways wind up with a bit - ter - sweet - heart,__

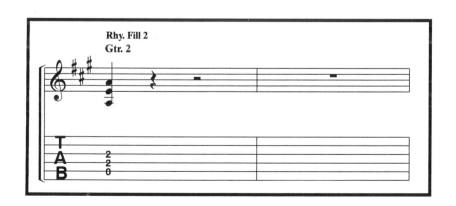

60

bit - ter - sweet - heart,_____

bit - ter - sweet - heart._____ In

*Both notes bend.

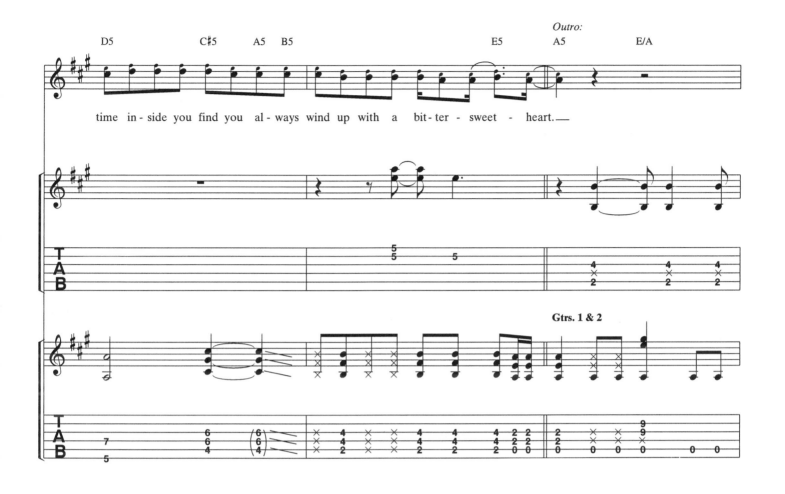

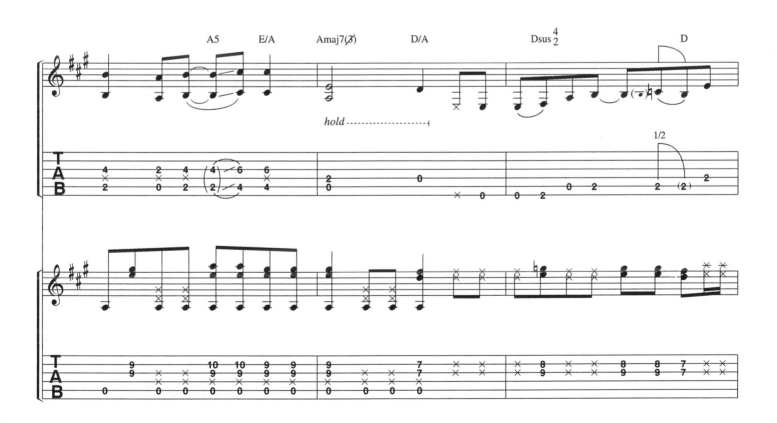

62

Verse 2:
It's like a suicide mission when you can't see no end.
Tired of compliment fishin' and impressin' your friends.
I never kissed no one just to kiss and tell.
It's a little bit of heaven and a whole lot of hell.
In the eye of the beholder is a beautiful start.
You always seem to end up with a bittersweetheart.
There's a darkness looming but the sun is shinin' bright,
I can live to see the morning if I stay up all night.

Chorus 2:
Bittersweetheart, bittersweetheart,
I've got to short cut, you got a head start.
Bittersweetheart, sad but it's true.
It's a bittersweetheart that's a hard heart to cure,
My bittersweetheart.

STRING OF PEARLS

By
DAVID PIRNER

70

swings   the string of pearls on the corn-er. The street-lights re-flect the light in the wa-ter. The

string,— it snaps,   and the pearls go   sail-ing and they splash and bounce and roll 'cross the wet street. As she

bends to chase the pearls, a car swings 'round the corn-er she darts from the eyes   of the pan-ic struck driv-er whose

rac-ing to   the de-liv-er-y room, 'cause in the back-seat, his wife is bust-in' out of her womb.—

String Of Pearls - 8 - 2
PG9541

String Of Pearls -8 - 3
PG9541

I can be-come the best pres-i-dent ev-er, and not just pres-i-dent,_ fend for your-self."_

(simile)

Moderately ♩ = 138

Chorus:

Oh._

Oh._

3. (He) signs his

end Riff B

*Allow last note of each part to ring into next section.

String Of Pearls - 8 - 7
PG9541

pros - ti - ute,   who was mis - sing   a pearl___ on the neck-

lace   that broke   late   last   night.___

Faster ♩ = 138
*w/Riffs **A** *(Gtr. 2)*, **B** *(Gtr. 3)*, & **Rhy. Fig. 1** *(Gtr. 5)*
Outro:

A   D   A

Gtr. 1

Oh. __
*Gtr. 4 tacet.

A   D   A

Repeat & fade

Oh. ___

Verse 4:
Now, his wife took the train to her ex-lover's funeral,
Who died in the bathroom, hit his head on a urinal.
When they got together, the knowledge was carnal,
And the widow was at the funeral
And they had quite a cat-fight.
And they fell into the hole where the casket was resting,
And the preacher just left in the middle of the service
'Cause death was one thing, but women made him nervous,
And he ran to his car and he drove 'round the corner.
(To Chorus:)

CRAWL

By
DAVID PIRNER and STEVE JORDAN

Crawl - 9 - 1
PG9541

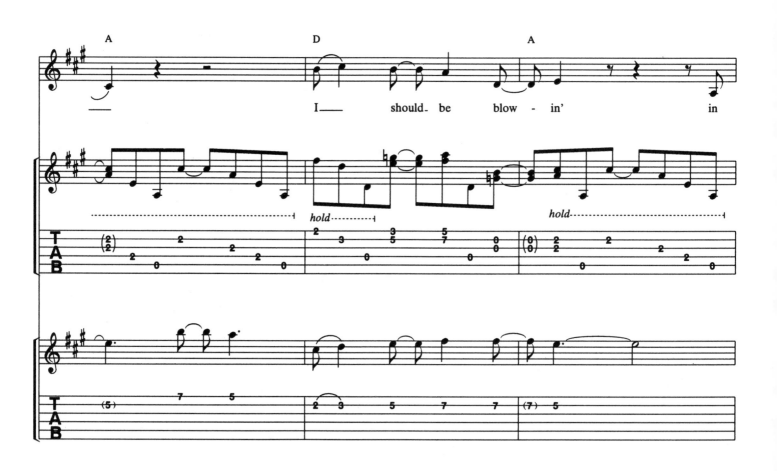

I— should be blow - in' in

To Coda

some - one— else - 's ear.— I'm look - ing for - ward to look -

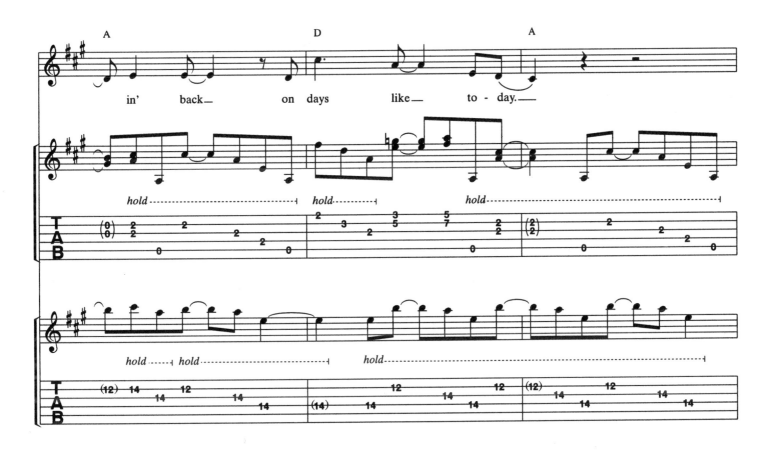

in' back— on days like— to - day.—

Though I wish— you'd go—— a - way,— stay, won't— you stay.—

80

crawl home, crawl home from here.

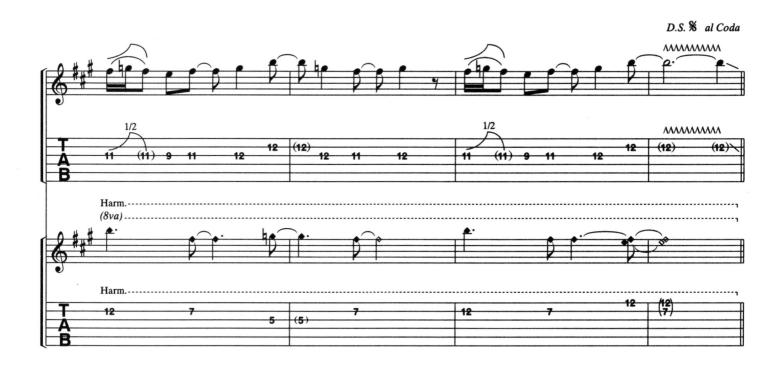

So get me___ out of here.   I

nev - er felt bet - ter just crawl - ing home.___ I'm gon - na crawl___ home,___

Crawl - 9 - 6
PG9541

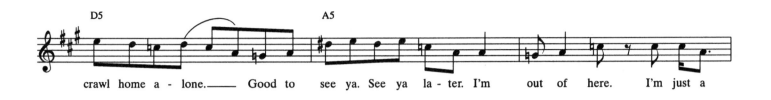

crawl home a - lone.___ Good to   see ya. See ya la - ter. I'm   out of here.   I'm just a

crawl___   home,___   a   crawl___   home___   from here.___

Outro:
w/Rhy. Fig. 2 *simile, (Gtr. 1) 3 times*

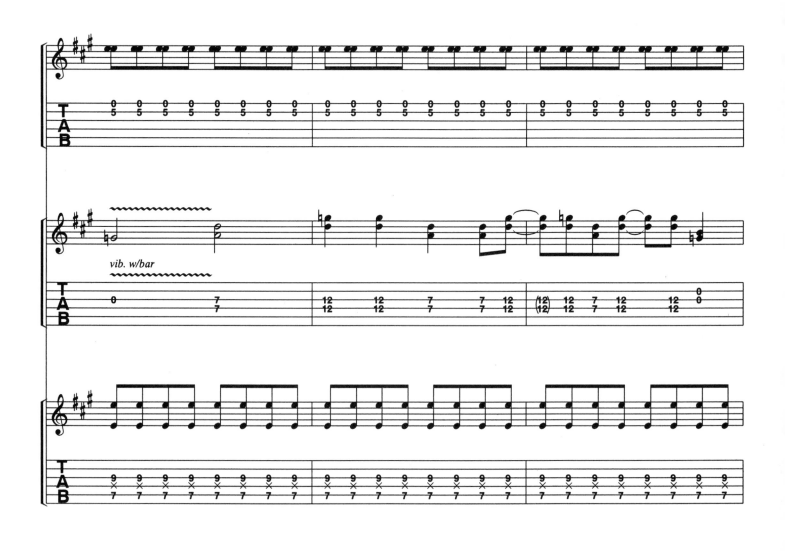

Verse 2:
Some respond to pleasure.
Some respond to pain.
I'm hanging out to dry
In the pouring rain.
Victims of temptation
Never can complain.
I could use the sensation, ya see
I can't feel pain.
(To Pre-chorus:)

Chorus 2:
I never ever said I'd never make it home.
It's just a stones throw, a crawl home.
Good to see ya.
See ya later.
Maybe one more beer.
I'm just a crawl home, a crawl home from here.

Verse 3:
I could use someone
To drag me out of here.
I am that someone.
It's all become quite clear.
Get me out of here.

CAGED RAT

By
DAVID PIRNER

Why don't you go home,— crawl in-to your hole?

*w/ad lib. sound effects and voices.

*w/bar pulling up.

*Keyboard arr. for gtr.

Caged Rat - 10 - 1
PG9541

Why don't you go home, spend some time a - lone?

1/4

1/4

hold----------------

N.C.(G5)

1. In the

Gtr. 2 out

end Rhy. Fig. 1

88

*Played simile on repeat.

Caged Rat - 10 - 3
PG9541

Caged Rat - 10 - 5
PG9541

Verse 2:
In the corner, in the, in the corner, in the, in the corner
I looked across the room.
I knew I'd be there soon,
In the corner.
(To Chorus)

EYES OF A CHILD

By
DAVID PIRNER

Eyes Of A Child - 8 - 1
PG9541

Eyes Of A Child - 8 - 6
PG9541

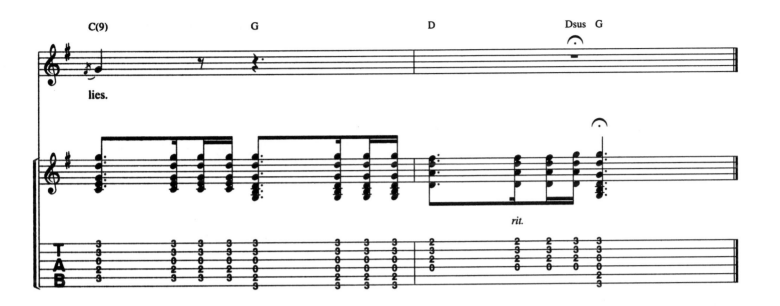

lies.

rit.

Verse 2:
He picked up the paper from the bitter cold morning.
He had just gone to sleep, he had to get up for work.
But by morning he's a watchman, by night he's a waiter,
In the late afternoon he works as a clerk.

Pre-Chorus 2:
And he can't pay the doctor bills, he just can't afford the pills.
The car's repossessed and the child support's due.

Chorus 2:
But he saw the world through the eyes of a child.
Big problems seem smaller and old things seem new.

Verse 3:
Well, she was just six when she turned her first trick,
And now she's thirteen and it don't make her sick.
And she does lots of crystal and she owns her own pistol,
Got a gold fish named Silver and a pimp who's named Rick.

Pre-Chorus 3:
And some are like customers and some are like patients.
She'd have gone back to school if she just had the patience.

Chorus 3:
But she saw the world through the eyes of a child,
None of the nightmares and nothing to deny.

JUST LIKE ANYONE

By
DAVID PIRNER

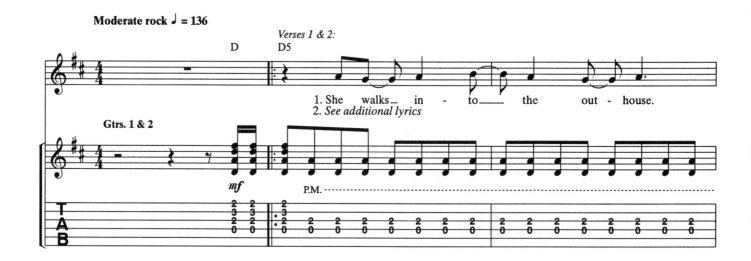

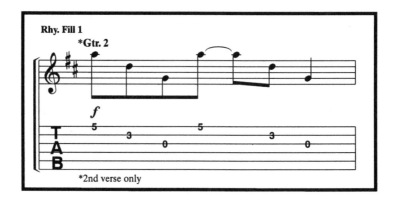

Just Like Anyone - 7 - 2
PG9541

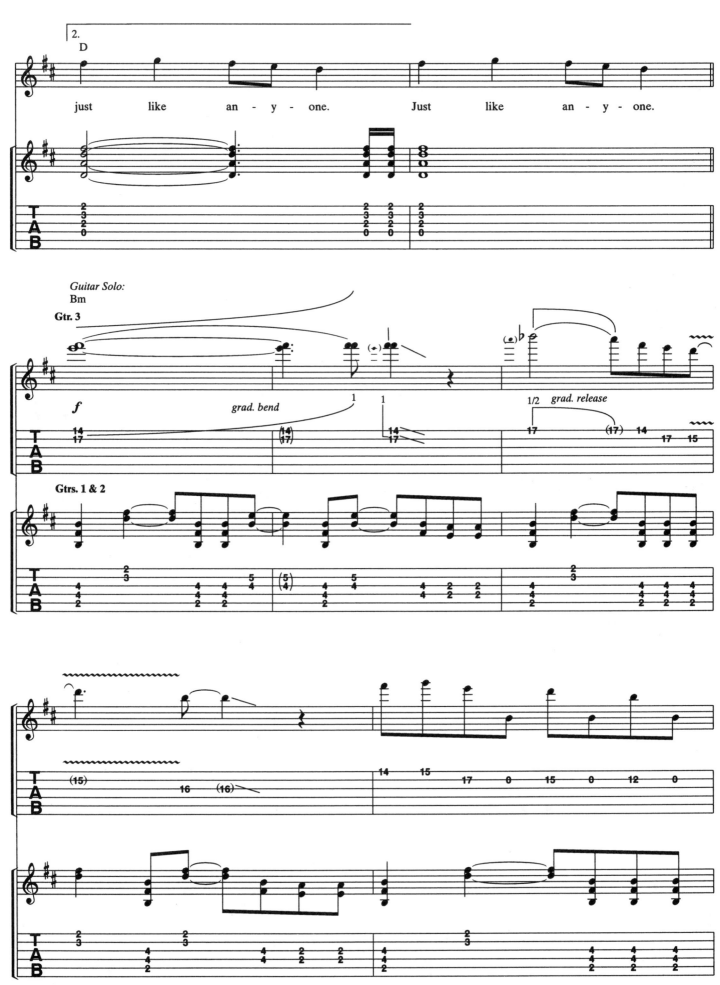

*Bass plays E.

108

110

wond-'ring what they mean, do they just mean to be mean? And think-ing a-bout the scene, do they

just want to be seen? Try not to seem so just like an-y-one.

(Just like an-y-one.

*Repeat and fade

Just like an-y-one.

Just like an-y-one.

Just like an-y-one.———)

Gtr. 1

Gtr. 2

Gtr. 3

*Vocal 1st time only.

*Add delay on repeats, set to high sustain.
During fade, gradually slow delay time.

Verse 2:
She reaches through the darkness.
Her fingers touch the porcelain seat.
She spins and pulls her pants down.
The cold air holds her like a thief.

Chorus 2:
And she starts wondering what they mean.
Do they just mean to be mean?
And thinking about the scene,
Do they just want to be seen?
Try not to seem so just like anyone,
Just like anyone.

TELL ME WHEN

By
DAVID PIRNER and L. SAMUELS

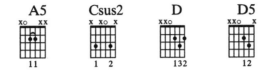

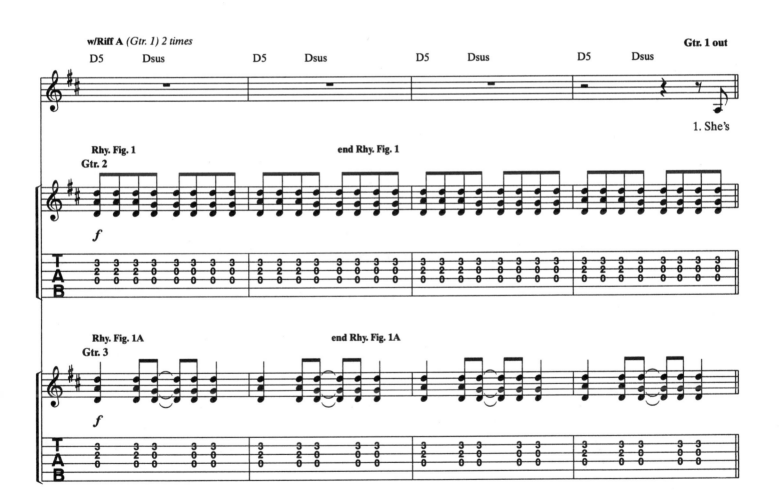

*w/dist. and E - Bow for sustain

Tell Me When - 10 - 1
PG9541

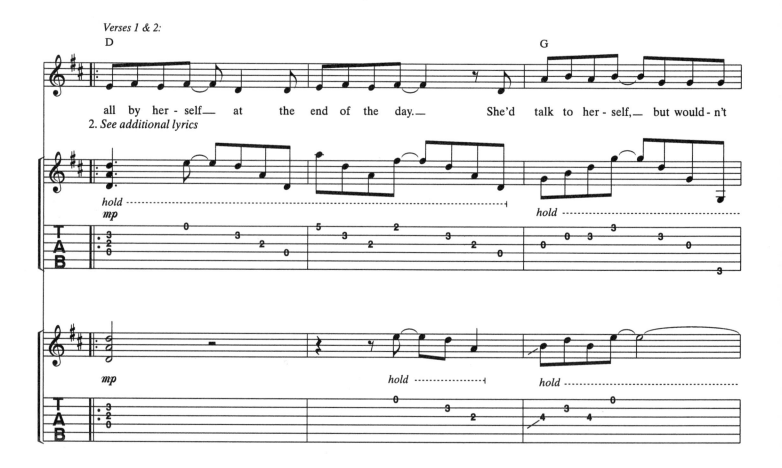

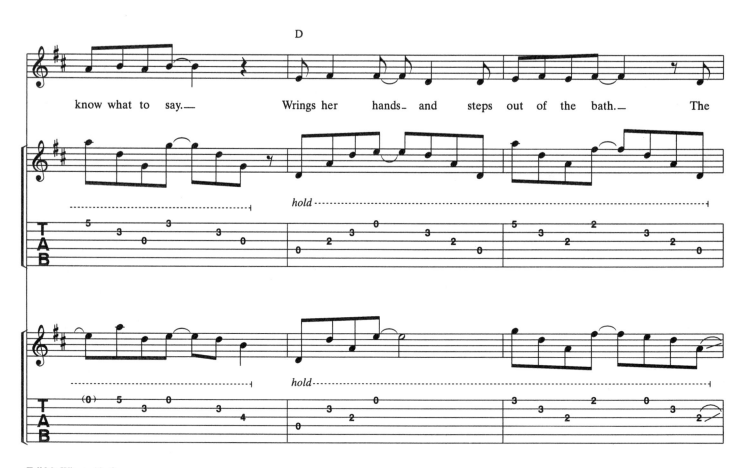

116

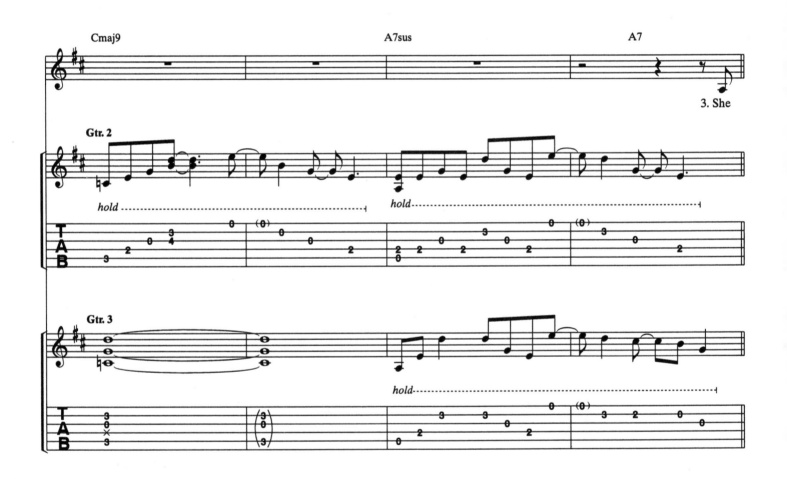

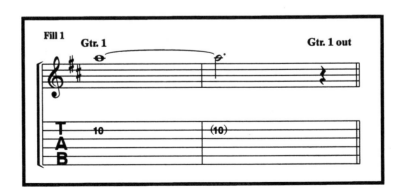

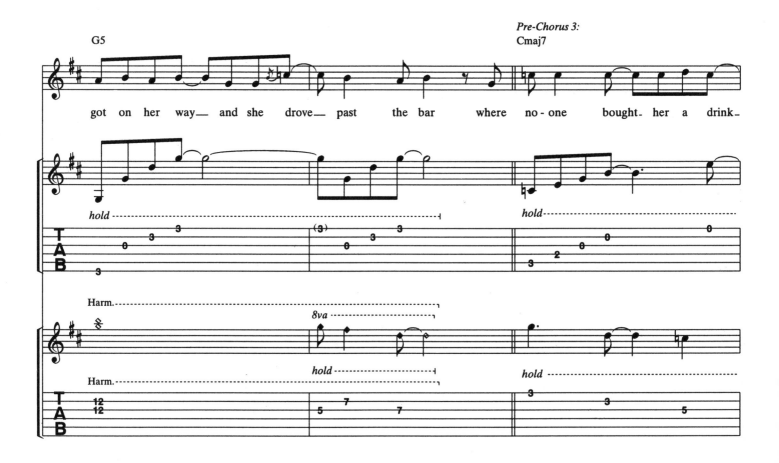

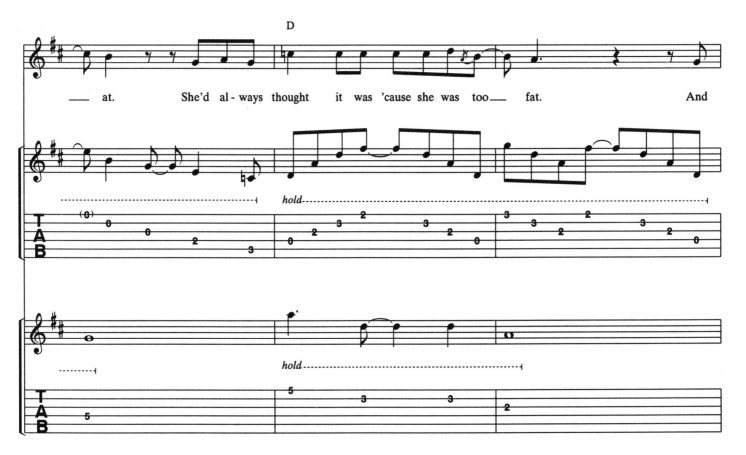

Cmaj7

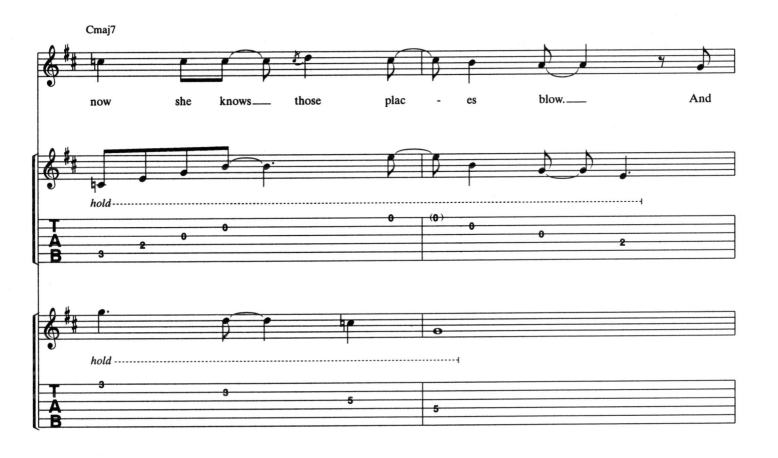

now   she   knows___   those   plac -   es   blow.___   And

D.S. ℅ al Coda

A7sus

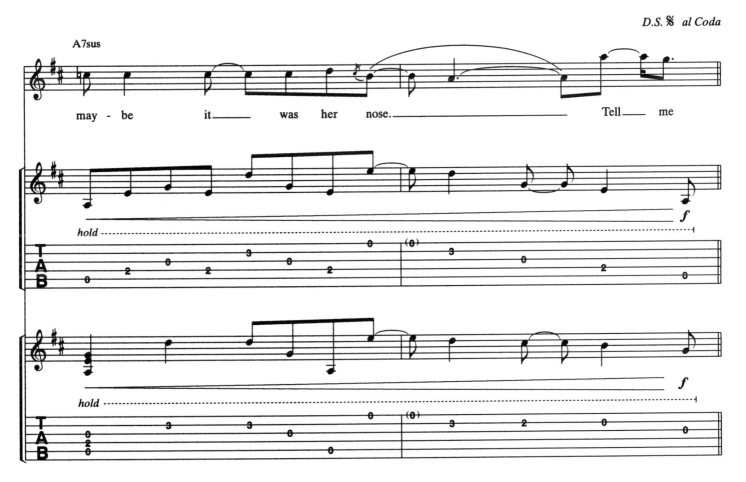

may - be   it___   was   her   nose.___   Tell___ me

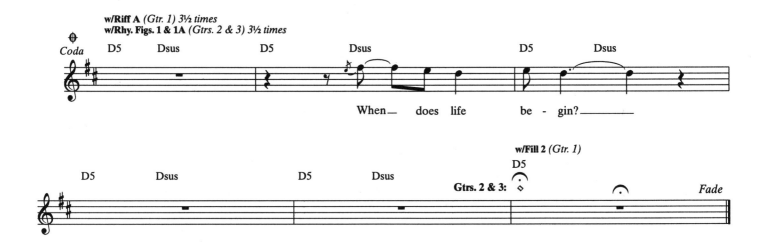

w/Riff A *(Gtr. 1) 3½ times*
w/Rhy. Figs. 1 & 1A *(Gtrs. 2 & 3) 3½ times*

Coda   D5   Dsus   D5   Dsus   D5   Dsus

When— does life be - gin?_____

w/Fill 2 *(Gtr. 1)*
D5   Dsus   D5   Dsus   D5   *Fade*

Gtrs. 2 & 3:

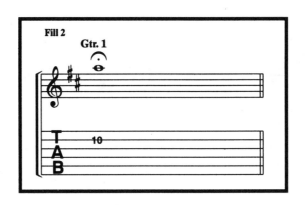

Fill 2
Gtr. 1

Verse 2:
She got in the car,
And looked up at the stars,
And made a wish.
She held her breath,
And considered death.

Pre-Chorus 2:
And in the rear-view mirror
She looked back on her reflection.
She was a long way
From where she wanted to be,
And a long way from perfection.

NOTHING TO WRITE HOME ABOUT

By
DAVID PIRNER

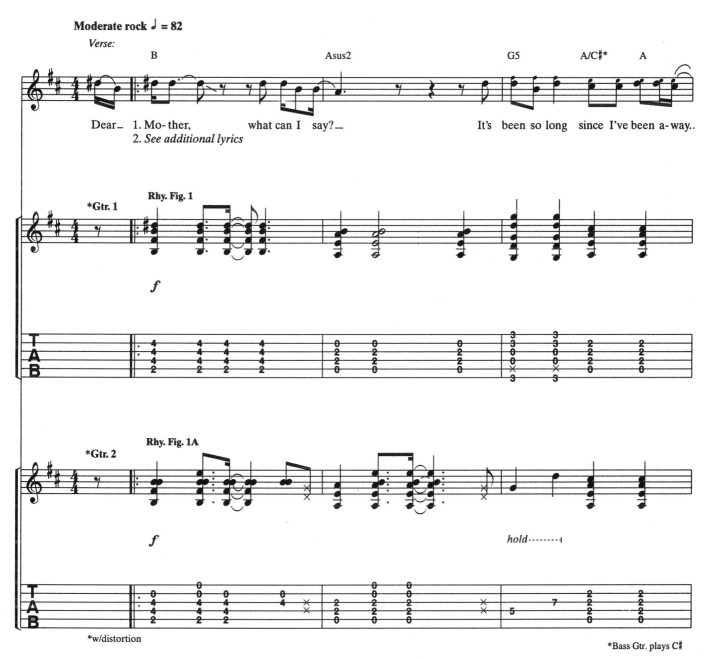

*w/distortion

*Bass Gtr. plays C#

Nothing to Write Home About - 8 - 1
PG9541

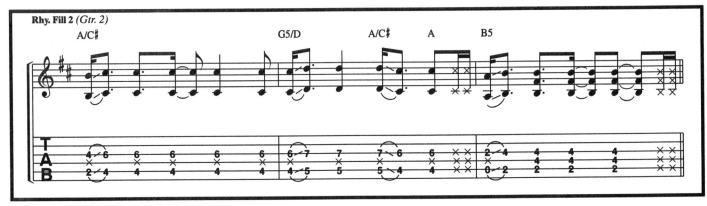

*Gtrs. 1 & 2 w/clean tone

126

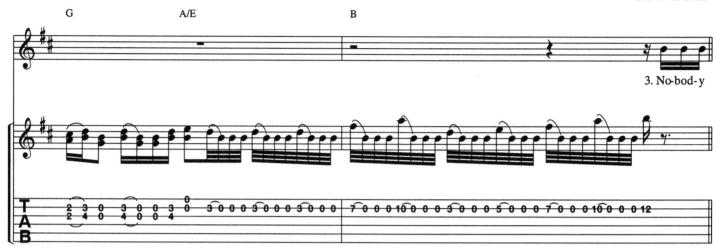

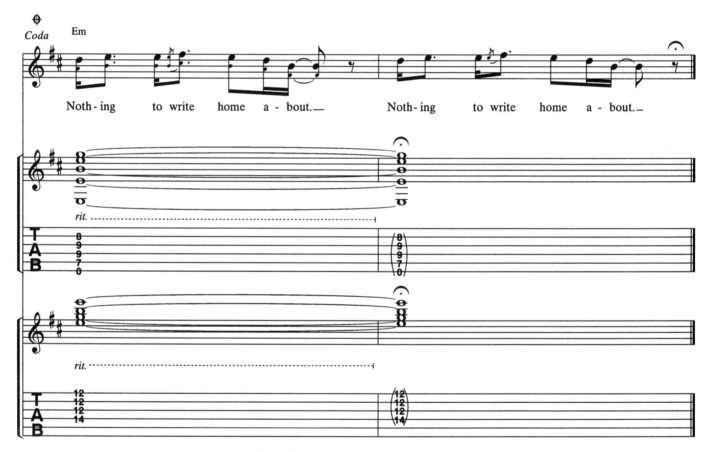

Verse 2:
Dear John, that ain't my name.
I'm just hangin' 'round to take the blame.
I'm filled with guilt, I'm filled with shame.
Too much or not enough, it's all the same.

Pre-Chorus 2:
No one wants to talk about the loss.
No one wants to talk about the cost.
And everyone just looks away
Just like any other day.
(To Chorus:)

Pre-Chorus 3:
Nobody told about any of this in school.
No one told me I'd be taken for a fool.
And everyone just looks away
And tries to make it throught the day.
(To Chorus:)

I DID MY BEST

By
DAVID PIRNER

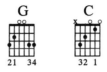

I Did My Best - 8 - 1
PG9541

*Three gtrs. arr. for one.

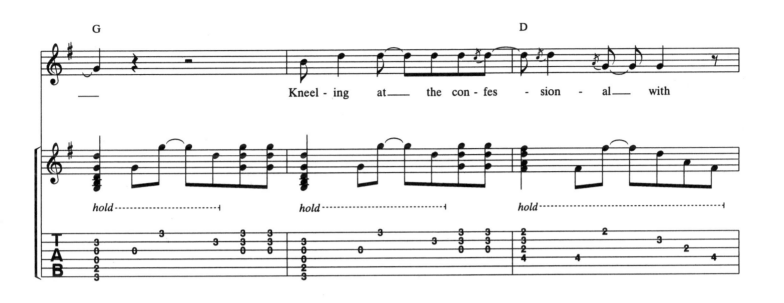

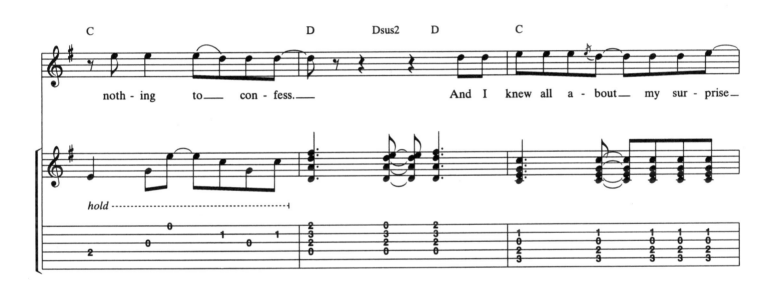

132

I Did My Best - 8 - 4
PG9541

134

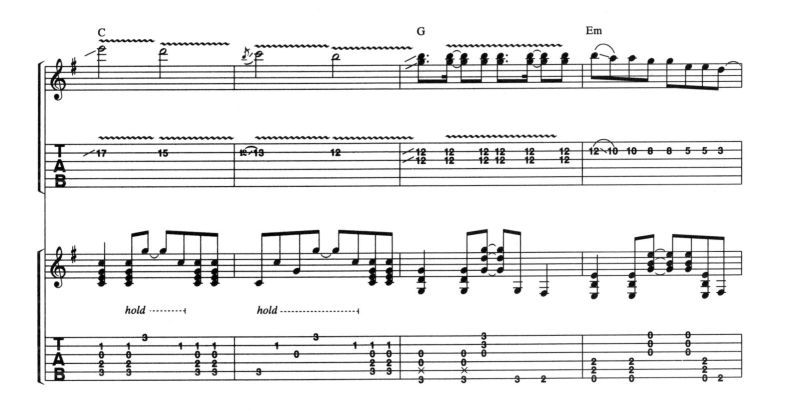

I Did My Best - 8 - 7
PG9541

136

I did my best for you.

Verse 2:
Stop the truck at the truck stop.
I need something to help me crash.
Food stamps, checks and credit cards
But they only accepted cash.
There was sweat beading on my brow
My heart was beating out of my chest.
So I stole everything they couldn't give away
Yes, I did my best.
To Chorus:

Verse 3:
I was waiting for a chain reaction
With a missing link.
Waiting for that trickle down
For ever circling the sink.
I was tired of being tired
I could not get no rest.
So I kept sleep walking and talking in my sleep.
Yes, I did my best.
To Chorus: